Copyright © 1993 Creative Editions.
123 South Broad Street, Mankato, MN 56001, USA
International copyrights reserved in all countries. No part of this book may
be reproduced in any form without written permission from the publisher.
Printed in Italy
Art Director: Rita Marshall
Book Design: Stephanie Blumenthal
Text Adapted and Edited from the French language by Kitty Benedict
Library of Congress Cataloging-in-Publication Data
Benedict, Kitty.
The oak/written by Andrienne Soutter-Perrot; adapted for the American reader
by Kitty Benedict; illustrated by Eleonore Schmid.
Summary: Describes the physical features of an oak tree, how it reproduces,
and where it grows.
ISBN 1-56846-040-6
1. Oak—Juvenile literature. [1. Oak. 2. Trees.]
I. Soutter-Perrot, Andrienne. II. Schmid, Eleonore, ill. III. Title.
QK495.F14B46   1992
583'.976--dc20   92-6003

THE OAK

WRITTEN BY

ANDRIENNE SOUTTER-PERROT

ILLUSTRATED BY

ELEONORE SCHMID

CREATIVE EDITIONS

WHAT IS AN OAK?

The oak is a large plant, a tree. Its many roots hold it tight in the ground. Its wide, strong trunk grows upward and spreads into long limbs.

The limbs split into smaller branches, out of which grow wavy-edged leaves. We say that these leaves are lobed.

The trunk and branches are protected by rough brown bark that cracks as the tree gets older. Oaks live a very long time. Some may live to be several hundred years old.

You can tell trees apart by their leaves, their bark, and the size and shape of their trunks. It is easy to see the difference between an oak and a birch tree.

HOW DOES THE OAK TREE LIVE?

Day and night, the oak tree breathes. Each leaf is full of microscopic holes that let air in and out.

The oak tree perspires, too. In summer, when the weather is hot and dry, the leaves give off water vapor which rises into the clouds.

Underground, the roots of the tree spread wide and deep. The smallest roots draw water and minerals from the soil, creating a transparent liquid that turns into sap.

The sap travels up to the leaves through thin tubes just beneath the bark, in the part of the tree called the sapwood.

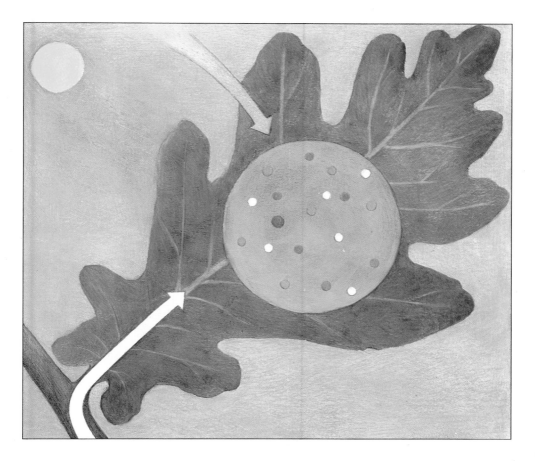

When the green leaves are exposed to light, they absorb a gas called carbon dioxide. They combine this gas with sap and turn it into food and oxygen.

The oxygen is released through tiny holes in the leaves. The food is carried through special tubes to the branches, trunk, and roots so that the tree can grow.

At the end of the summer, small green cones appear at the bases of the leaves and the tips of the branches.

Year after year, the sapwood grows new tubes for carrying food.
This is how the trunk and branches get bigger and thicker.

Between the sapwood and the center of the trunk, old tubes gradually block up. Sap no longer reaches this part of the tree. It has turned into wood.

When an oak is cut down, you can see rings in the wood. Each ring represents one year's growth. To find out the age of a tree, all you need to do is count the number of rings, starting from the center.

HOW DOES THE OAK TREE REPRODUCE?

Each spring, little rounded buds sprout on
the tips of the branches. New yellow-green
leaves fan out from these buds.

Every year or two, the buds produce flowers along with the leaves.
The tiny, odorless flowers hang on slender stalks.

The yellowish blooms are the male flowers, called catkins. The female flowers are light red, and fewer in number.

The slightest breeze makes the catkins release billions of tiny golden grains, called pollen.

When a grain of pollen lands on a female flower, it slowly grows into an acorn.

At the end of summer, the acorns are ripe. Each shiny case conceals a nut.

In the fall, the sap runs more slowly through the tree. The acorns fall
and the leaves dry out and turn brown. In the winter, the tree hardly
looks alive.

In the spring, the earth grows warm again and the tree awakens.
Nearby, a tiny root breaks through the tip of a fallen acorn. The root
burrows into the ground.

A stem appears, with a bud and two leaves. If it gets enough sun and rain, this baby oak will grow larger every year.

WHERE DO OAK TREES GROW?

Oak trees grow best in places where it is not too hot and not too cold. They may stand alone in pastures, or be grouped with other trees in the woods or along the roads.

A thousand years ago, immense oak forests grew in America and in Europe. Many animals found food and shelter in them.

Most of these forests have disappeared. The trees were cut down, and wheat, grain, and corn were planted in their place.

Oak was the hardwood used to build the framework of cathedrals and the hulls of sailing ships. Today it is a rare and expensive wood.

Oak trees are a valuable resource for us all.